HELIGAN

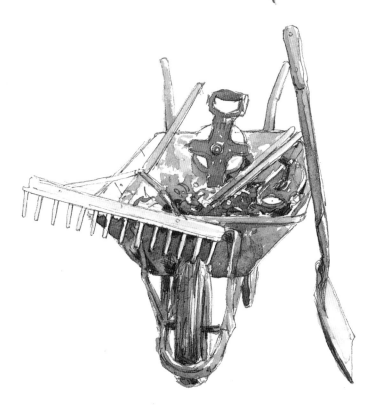

~ a celebration

Published by
Truran
Croft Prince
Mount Hawke
Truro
Cornwall TR48EE
www.truranbooks.co.uk

Printed by -
R. Booth   at the
Troutbeck Press
Antron Hill
Mabe , Penryn
Cornwall TR109HH

ISBN   1 85022 156 1 (cased)
ISBN   1 85022 155 3 (Paperback)

The gardens are open all year round .

The Lost Gardens of Heligan , Pentewan , St. Austell , Cornwall , PL266EN .
Tel: 01726845100   www.heligan.com

The first thing I notice about Heligan is evidence of hard work everywhere...

The Hidden Valley - Winter

pheasants croaking & squirrels everywhere
& don't have many trees at home - &   I love to see them like this -
                                        bare & sharp against the sky.

5

The Mud Maid, sleeping in the winter.
I didn't mean her to spread over two pages, but she
refused to fit into one...

6

winter - the sounds of sawing
& the smell of bonfires

And drifts of
snowdrops in Janry

... and rain, rain & more rain ...

9

a perfect leaf on the jungle boardwalk

It's hard to eat anything without sharing it...

And they make the BEST date slices here!

under the vines

one white feather shining out among the autumn grasses

Bits & pieces

10

Lacework draincovers . . . .

started drawing the outside of this one
but as I get nearer the centre I can see it is the same as
the one above!!

11

summer & winter — looking across the pond & up to the house from the top of the jungle

12

And ... the wibbly, wobbly tree ...

13

the first periwinkle flowers & a ladybird
- very early spring

cyclamen, tiny & delicate, in the litter of
dead leaves

14

daffodils   by the bee boles
Are they "Pentewan"?

The Handkerchief tree - with huge handkes!
where the branch dips into the shelter of the
walled garden

Furry magnolia buds opening...

Theres a fatter, darker pink/mauve-
budded tree on the other side of the
vegetable garden

How can I choose just a few from all the
camellias & rhododendrons (did I spell that right?)
of every colour from white through palest pink to deep red & mauve

The bee boles.

I've seen the squirrels & birds enjoying all this alone ... well, apart from the gardeners; on a June day the hum of conversation joins the birdsong

16

There are still some corners where the old walls stand unrestored... & just as beautiful.

In fact — it's hard to tell the difference.

17

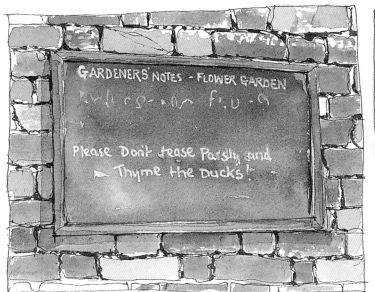

GARDENERS' NOTES - FLOWER GARDEN

Please Don't tease Parsly and
Thyme the Ducks!

Gardeners' notes . . .

GARDENERS' NOTES - MELON YARD

MELON HOUSE - Full of seedlings
DARK ROOM - Mushrooms
BOTTOM FRAME - Hardening off
early peas

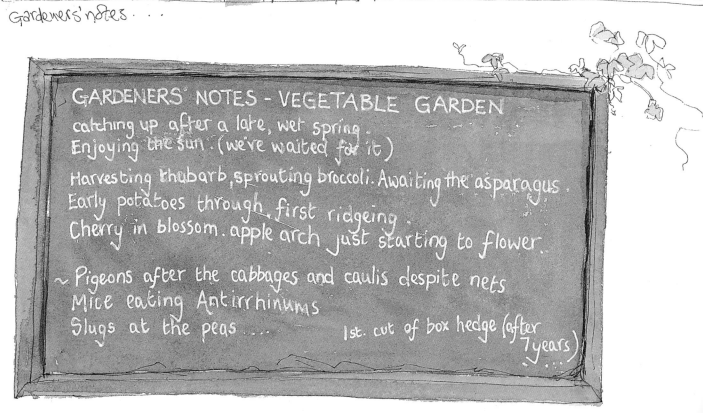

GARDENERS' NOTES - VEGETABLE GARDEN
catching up after a late, wet spring.
Enjoying the sun. (we've waited for it)

Harvesting rhubarb, sprouting broccoli. Awaiting the asparagus.
Early potatoes through, first ridging.
Cherry in blossom. apple arch just starting to flower.

~ Pigeons after the cabbages and caulis despite nets
Mice eating Antirrhinums
Slugs at the peas . . .   1st. cut of box hedge (after 7 years)

All the different mints are coming up in their beds in the Melon Yard — Apple, Corsican, eau de cologne, ginger, lavender, Moroccan, Pineapple, Red

Moroccan

Boots in the potting shed

In the Melon yard .

Full of seedlings in the spring. then strawberries melons pineapples tomatos bursting out of frames.

20

21

I'm having a crisis... How can I
do this justice??
There are bluebells, violets
primroses, campions, celandines
speedwell, herb robert,
buttercups, new ferns,
small white flowers,
creeping yellow ones,
others in bud just about
to burst, new leaves on every
tree, lily of the valley,
white starry flowers,
tiny blue ones...
light changing by the second.
Then theres the abstract things,
the birdsong, the peace,
the scents & smells...
! forgot the honeysuckle WHY DO I EVEN TRY...

time to fluff a cup of coffee

23

Transplanting seedlings
24

netted peas

sticking the peas

Nothing peas; trenching celery
of bean poles up.

PEA
Veitch's Western Express

GALES, RAIN, HAIL, SLUGS

BROAD BEAN
Aguadulce

The first flowers on the broad beans

25

Winter

Summer

The apple arch - the lady of the house could walk through
surrounded by blossoms sweet scents - not cabbages &
manure ...

26

spring

the Rev. w. Wilkes & Arthur Turner are both looking gorgeous... in blossom on the apple arch... in May.

and I can't remember which is which!

27

The bottom of the jungle, wind beginning to roar in the tops of the trees

The top of the jungle Thunder rumbling

29

something strange in the water

Tall pink flowers with just the tiniest leaves right at the bottom

"things" from the jungle — which grows as you watch it

Giant Rhubarb

30

the tree ferns have curly new shoots at
the top just like all the other ferns .

31

A very handsome rooster with some of his hens

In the summer the geese are in amongst the fruit trees. They look wonderful & I now have a vision of white geese in our orchard at home. (but then I have visions of lots of things ...) Reality usually overtakes... In the form of mud, brambles, & hens & other people's veg. patches!

This looks just like my china chicken dish on the dresser at home.. but it is a real dove...

each time I visit I hear the pheasants, but rarely see them close up.

They are so exotic & beautiful...

33

Inside the potting shed. · It's always cool &
quiet in here.

SAVING
for
SEED

Different flowers every time
I visit.
Seed drying, plants hanging
to dry onions, mushrooms
The old hurricane lamp had mistletoe
turned round it at Christmas.

Forking manure into the pineapple pit
I saw a wren perched in one of the
spaces in the brick wall—I wonder
if they nest in there?

35

from manure & straw & tiny shoots

to thick undergrowth in August

The rhubarb patch with its wonderful what are they? forcing pots?

36

And the giant rhubarb - looking wonderful in June - & battered by the first
Autumn gales

The bananas are huge & green &
lovely - & fruiting

But in the winter they are dead -
do they really grow back from these
brown & shrivelled things?

Digging & planting

Raking, hoeing, weeding
planning, pruning

Sawing & burning

Picking, cleaning,
washing

38

Pushing & pulling, hauling &
lifting
Stacking, drying, hanging & tying

rain & hail,
wind & sun
The work NEVER stops!

39

Hot, Summer days

sweet peas & lots of daisy-type flowers.

40

thyme & tansy, lemon balm, sage, fennel, parsley, chives, rosemary
marjoram, salad burnet | Marsh mallow, lavender, coriander, basil
bergamot

sunbathing in the orchard . .

A banana tree lives in solitary state
in a house by the walled flower garden —
much larger & greener than those that
take their chances in the jungle.

— And the other side of the wall—
the vine house (r I think our
grapes were bigger last year !!)

43

"And the Melon yard...

Autumn in the veg garden

LEAF BEET
LEAF ROQA
CABBAGE

45

The head gardener's office is always full of goodies, drying flowers & row upon row of saved seeds in the autumn.

CARROT SUTTON KIN
CABBAGE DURHAM EARLY
Meteor
LINKOLN
PEAS
CABBAGE SNOWBALL
LARKSPUR

The compost heap in the vegetable garden - November. Halloween pumpkins, grape peashucks, bean pods, old vegetables, leave

And... Always... wheelbarrows, everywhere.

47

I need more, pages, more time, another year. I want to work in the vegetable garden - not digging - painting . . . .

There's fruit to draw, all the wild flowers I've missed, harvest colours to paint. I haven't put the farm walk in, r the animals. I need more reflections r exotic foliage from the jungle. And what about all the glasshouses? The peach blossom? the orange trees? The Italian garden, the straw bed in the loft above the thunderbox. The view of the Gribben from the Northern summerhouse . . . I haven't drawn a pineapple or a melon. I haven't described the different scents at different times of year, or the rooks cawing in winter trees . . it goes on . . . r on . . . .
r on .